Echoes, Edges & Epiphanies

Reflections from a Sailor's Soul

Commander V Srivatan

BookLeaf Publishing
India | USA | UK

Made with ❤ on the BookLeaf Publishing Platform
www.bookleafpub.in
www.bookleafpub.com

Dedication

For my *Appa*, **Shri R Varadarajan** & my father-in-law,
Wg Cdr S. M. Singh -
two men who could recite *Shakespeare, Keats, Tennyson, Ghalib* & *Khusro* at will -
but never had the pleasure of quoting me.
This one's for you!

And to **Safina**, my compass & my calm & my anchor –
this book is as much yours as it is mine!

Preface

After decades at sea as an officer in the Indian Navy & thereafter navigating the shifting tides of the private sector - charting courses across ninety-odd countries - I've gathered these poems like shells from distant shores. Each holds an echo of experience, teeters on the edge of understanding, or emerges from a quiet epiphany.

The title, ***Echoes, Edges & Epiphanies***, surfaced naturally. The echoes reflect universal truths that ripple across cultures - the same laughter in a Viennese café sounds remarkably like joy in a Mumbai *bazaar*. The edges mark life's inevitable thresholds: between youth & wisdom, presence & absence, holding on & letting go. And the epiphanies are those sudden clearings in the fog - brief moments when life's patterns reveal themselves with unexpected clarity.

Yet, as this collection grew from a handful of poems to a full century, so too did its horizons expand. What began as a reflection on shared humanity evolved into a more layered journey - one that charts not merely the external landscapes of countries & cultures, but the internal terrain of the human spirit.

These verses delve deeper, speaking not only of what unites us but also of what fractures us - the relentless tug-of-war between hope & despair, belonging & alienation, permanence & transience. *The Ballad of the Infodemic IDIOT* wrestles with the absurdity of our modern information age, while *The Ever-Retreating Tomorrow* captures the tragicomic dance between ambition & procrastination. *The Shrinking Shopping Bag* holds a quiet meditation on ageing & loss, even as *Pawsome Economics* revels in the uncomplicated wisdom of canine contentment. These poems span from the grand stage of cultural confluence to the intimate corners of nostalgia, longing & resilience.

In crafting these reflections, I have attempted to navigate the vast waters of human experience - charting both its tempests & its calm, its familiar harbours & uncharted depths. After a lifetime of reading nautical charts, I now attempt to map the emotional landscapes that connect us all.

Whether you sail thru' this collection from bow to stern or let the currents carry you where they may, I hope these poems echo within you, illuminate your edges & perhaps spark an epiphany of your own.

~ *A retired sailor, still navigating the deeper oceans of human experience*

Acknowledgements

These verses wouldn't have been achieved unless thru' the inspirational guidance of two exceptional individuals - my late father, ***Shri R Varadarajan*** & my late father-in-law, ***Wg Cdr SM Singh***.

I developed an abiding love affair with the English language thru' my father - its nuances became a playground I explored without formal training. He instilled in me the secret of the '***3As***' - **A***rresting Beginning*, **A***bsorbing Middle & Finish with an* **A***plomb* - principles that have shaped my writing & remain his enduring legacy.

From my father-in-law, I inherited a deep appreciation for poetry, both in English & Urdu. His effortless recitation of verses from *Shakespeare, Keats, Tennyson, Blake, Mirza Ghalib & Amir Khusro* was nothing short of inspirational, a trait he shared with my father. Only, where they quoted the greats, I longed to quote my own. Their love for poetry left an indelible mark on me - not just as a reader, but as someone determined to contribute his own voice to the chorus of verse.

My deepest gratitude goes to my wife, ***Safina*** - my anchor. Her unwavering belief, love & patience have been the bedrock of my journey, allowing me to navigate the seas of creativity with confidence. To my children, ***Tamanna*** & ***Armaan***, your constant support & love have been my companions thru' every tide & tempest.

I owe a special debt to ***Mrs. Kamala Bhuvarahan***, my senior school English teacher, who, in perfect harmony with my father, nurtured my love for the language. Her faith in my potential often exceeded my own, planting a seed that has since taken root & flourished in these pages. She cultivated not just my grasp of grammar & prose but a deep appreciation for the rhythm of words - a gift that continues to shape my writing today.

Over two decades in the Indian Navy, & later in the corporate world, I had the privilege of learning from uniformed personnel & a diverse array of individuals across nationalities. They instilled in me the discipline of thought & the art of translating observations, feelings & emotions into words. A special mention goes to ***Commodore Srikant Kesnur***, whose elegant prose has long been a source of inspiration, pushing me to pursue greater clarity & grace in my writing.

To the countless souls who have touched my life - whether thru' fleeting encounters or enduring bonds - you are all woven into the fabric of these poems. Every experience, every shared moment, has left its mark.

And finally, to you, dear ***Reader***, thank you for allowing these words to resonate in your heart. It is in your reflection that these poems truly come alive!

The Calendar Doesn't Lend You Wisdom

I've watched them count their wrinkles like medals,
Each year a badge they wear with hollow pride-
As if December's passing grants them sight
Beyond what August knew. How strange to think
That turning pages makes one somehow wise!

I've seen them wield their age like royal sceptres,
Commanding reverence for time served alive,
While wisdom sits, a wallflower at their feast,
Watching them spoon-feed prejudice to youth
And call it "***experience***" or "***time-earned truth***!"

My neighbour counts his birthdays religiously,
Yet still believes the earth is somehow flat.
His grandson, barely twelve, corrects his math
With patience that the old man never learned.
Tell me: which one has truly grown up here?

They say that wine improves with passing time,

But humans aren't cabernet in caves -
Some souls turn vinegar in ageing barrels,
While others stay as grape juice all their days,
Too sweet & simple for complexity!

I've met bright children with old souls inside,
And ancient fools who never learned to share.
The calendar's a neutral chronicler
That merely counts our orbits round the sun,
Indifferent to the wisdom we might gain!

So spare me all your "***back in my day***" tales,
Your tenure in this world grants no degree
In living well or seeing clearly now.
The only wisdom worth its weight in gold
Is earned thru' growth, not merely growing old!

So check your calendar, count if you must
The days you've breathed this planet's thinning air,
But wisdom's not a vessel idly moored -
It's earned thru' storms & calms, thru' depths unknown,
Thru' charts we draw with open hearts & minds.
Like ancient mariners who learned to read
The stars above, not just count passing days,
True wisdom navigates life's shifting seas
With compass points of empathy & grace,
While mere age drifts, anchorless in time's bay!!!

Hey, "Almost"

You're that weird space right before victory,
Where success is so close you can **almost** taste it,
But somehow slips thru' your fingers like sand,
Leaving you with nothing but a bitter laugh
And a whole lot of "***what-if***" floating around.

Every single day, you're that **almost**-but-not-quite moment,
The near-miss that drives us totally crazy -
A job interview where you were this close,
The perfect comeback you think of later,
The dream that's always just out of reach.

Seriously, "**Almost**"? You're that annoying friend
Who shows up uninvited, hangs around just enough
To remind us how close we were to winning,
Then vanishes, leaving nothing but potential
And a whole lot of frustrated energy!!!

Pawsome Economics: A Study in Canine Contentment

My dog awaits me, grinning at the door-
not once has he inquired about my stocks.
He does not mind the car I drive, nor ask
if leather seats are warmer than regret!

He eats his meals with faith, not fuss or flair -
no Michelin-star critique, no diet fads.
A stick, a shoe, a leaf - each one a prize!
(*No quarterly reports on market trends*)

At night, he sighs & curls up by my feet,
his tail content with being here, not more.
He does not chase promotions, dream of yachts,
or check for likes before he wags his joy.

I tell him humans measure worth in weight-
of metal, paper, pixels, passing trends.

He tilts his head, as if to say, "***But why?***"
Then licks my face, 'coz he loves me still!!!

An Ode to my Muse

Oh! Thou selfish Muse
Why art thou flown away?
Wherefore have I wronged you?
Sit I with my pen & paper,
for drawing a pen-picture,
of Man or mountain,
The flora or the fauna,
The mind of Man or his busy nothings.
But where art thou & why
Desert me,
Leaving me pensive & petulant?

I'm no painter
That I should daub anything
With an easel & box of paints
Standing by in mute attendance.
I shan't tempt you
On the strength of Bacchus
For I touch not spirituous potions.
I can make no flight of fancy

On the wings of poesy
For I am no Keats!

Trust I myself to my pen
And paper & **YOU** -
If you elude who shall I turn to?
Together we make a page devastating,
Alone I am only vegetating.
So stay by me & with me stay
Give me succour & give me support
And let me have my say!!!

Do You Know?

Do you know
how difficult it is
to sleep at night,
knowing
that the same lovely stars above me
are also shining down on you,
close as a whisper & a lifetime apart?

Do you know
how difficult it is
to sleep at night
when I cannot wait to wake
& walk again, the same earth
that you, across the miles,
are impressing with your footsteps?

Do you know
how difficult it is
to sleep at night,
listening

to the howling wind beyond the walls,
& knowing that the same wind
carries your sweet Breath?

Do you know
how easy it would be
to sleep forever
if you
& I
could be together
if only in a dream???

Why I Love You

If asked why I love her I would say
It's the sway in her hips,
the leanness in her thighs.
It's the lust in her lips,
the love in her eyes.
It's the softness of her skin,
the silk in her hair.
It's the twist in her walk.
the sweetness in her talk.
It's the way she loves me
that makes me love her each day.
That is what I would say!!!

Life...

The glorious uncertainties
That life does deal in
Sometimes benign, sometimes not so.
The dice - it rolls in strange patterns
From the lowly 2 to the max dozen
Filling us with nadirs & zeniths new
'Twas one such roll
Which brought you close
Traversed a thousand days
In the blink of an eye
Breathtaking pace - comforting...
And at the same time discomforting...
Am I strong enough to deal
With this whole new dimension
Of having someone like you,
Pure of thought, purer of intention
But a crazy roller-coaster sans any tension?
Ease with which we connect & remain so
Smacks of life's ironical blow
Let's see how these two deal with this

Is what it seems to be saying - don't miss.
I'm tempted to consider it a providential blow
That it is YOU unbridled, that I get to know!

Self-Contradiction

Be it a friend or foe
When one is in woe,
The heart goes out to him.
There is a well of sympathy
Which overflows when kindled.

Only that none can understand
How the members of the human race
Possessing such fine & sentiments lofty
Bring themselves to kill wantonly,
To decimate its own kind.

The animals but kill in fear
Or when they are hungry.
But we forge new weapons
O' destruction to end ourselves.
Isn't it a paradox?
We kill the many in order
That a few may survive?

Would existence bearable be
If the earth contaminated became
And those that outlive would lead
Lives as vegetables?
Their life-force quenched by the fire
They did ignite.

Man! Thou art at the crossroads.
Who shall tell thee to live
& let live?
Dost, thou dream, I repeat, that others
Die that thou may live forever?
Call it illusion or self-delusion
Thou should'st decide betimes -
IT'S NOW OR NEVER
AMEN!

Jet Age or Progress

Time was when man met man
As one of his own kind
Full of fellow-feeling & love.

He listened & shared
And felt that the worries of one
Were the worries of the other.

He had the leisure to stand in wait,
To take hold of the crying child &
Stomp, play & jump about.

Gone are those days - What???
Those were the good 'ol days!!!
When shall come the like again?

Man in now ever on the move
As tho' driven by some force unseen,
Stop him by the shoulder
And ask what his hurry & haste is 'bout

He will blink & wink
Poor man, he has no time to think!!!

The Gravity of Growing Up

Scraped

At seven, the world was gravel:
knees bloomed crimson carnations,
saltwater prayers hissed thru' teeth,
and dirt clung like a catechism.
We wore scabs as medals,
picked at them like loose theology -
- believing skin, at least, could mend!

Bruised

By thirty, the wounds go nomadic:
they slip beneath the ribcage's vault,
map fractures across the mind's wet clay.
A lover's silence splits the sternum,
a friend's blade masquerades as a tongue.
The heart, that clumsy origami,
folds itself into smaller, stranger shapes!

We build altars to our own naiveté -
kneel not to gods, but to the ghosts

of who we thought we'd be.
The brain, a struck bell, hums
with the aftershock of every almost!

Epilogue

Funny, isn't it?
We've traded gravel for gravity,
yet still mistake the falling
for flight!!!

Confluence of the Infinite

Beneath the sun's first gold, a nation stirs -
a breath, a pulse, a billion footfalls drawn
to where three sacred rivers braid their light.
Prayagraj awakes, her banks now throbbing
with the hum of *Sankalp*, of chants that rise
like incense-smoke to pierce the waking sky.
Thirty crore souls - a human Ganga - flow
thru' dust & dawn, their faces turned as one
toward the holy dip, that ancient promise:
Here, the waters remember!

Saffron flames - *sadhus, naga babas* - march,
their ash-clad bodies mapping constellations
older than these shores. The air vibrates
with conch-shell hymns, with bells that tremble
as if the earth herself were ringing.
Mothers clasp infants, elders limp on hope,
youths bear grandparents on their backs - all merge
into this tide, this momentary melting
of caste, of tongue, of time!

Night falls, but the riverbank still shimmers -
a galaxy of tents, of lanterns strung
like prayers between the stars. Voices weave
a fabric of dialects: Tamizh, Bhojpuri, German,
Nepali, French - the world's breath mingling
where Gods & mortals meet. Even the moon
bends low, a silver vessel pouring grace
on heads anointed, sins dissolved to froth!

And when the crowd thins, when the last hymn fades,
the sand retains their footprints - countless, nameless -
etched into the silt like sacred script.
For this is no mere gathering, but proof:
how faith can turn a river into a mirror,
reflecting all who dare to drown themselves
in something vast, unyielding, alive.
A pilgrimage not just of place, but scale -
where humanity, for once, outnumbers fear!!!

The Unsolvable

In daily rhythms, we seek answers, cures -
A balm for every scrape upon our souls.
We plot & plan to mend each fraying thread,
Convinced that every knot can be undone.
A child's tears, a lover's doubt, the ache
Of time-worn bonds between once-close siblings:
We google quick solutions, ten-step guides,
As if all hearts were puzzles to unlock.

In board rooms, corner offices, we chart
The course to victory, to be the best.
We crunch the numbers, optimise, refine,
Believing excellence can be distilled.
Yet some things slip between our grasping hands:
The wordless distance growing year by year,
The fading light within a friend's tired eyes,
The hunger that no feast can satisfy.

We overthink each choice, each path, as if
The perfect option waits, if we just search.

But life defies our neat categorisation,
And wisdom often lies in letting go.
Not every problem has a tidy fix,
Not every wound will heal without a scar.
In acceptance of life's ragged edges,
We might find peace amidst the unsolved mess!!!

This Will Do

The thrift store sweater, frayed at both cuffs,
holds the warmth of someone else's skin.
I slip it on, ignore the newer racks -
"***This will do***," I tell the mirror's doubt!

My neighbour brings tomatoes from her vine,
their skins split red, too ripe to keep long.
I slice the bruises out, resist the urge
to buy a dozen more at the *subzi mandi.*
The pulp tastes sweeter for its imperfection!

The couch sags where we've carved our nightly shapes,
the coffee table scarred by careless cups.
No catalogues of leather, chrome, or oak
can shame this nest of lived-in ordinary.
We watch the lamp flicker - let it flicker!

A text arrives: ***You're missing out. Come live!***
The party's glow spills thru' my darkened screen.
I mute the chat, delete the app, then trace

the moon's thin curve, a thumbnail of light.
This will do, I tell the restless air!

The promotion passed me by again last spring.
My desk stays cluttered, but the bills are paid.
I water plants that never quite bloom,
admire their stubborn green, the way they lean
toward what's sufficient. ***Let them lean!***

No bucket lists, no bucketful of stars -
just laundry folded, footpaths memorised,
the postman's nod, the kettle's steady plea.
I stir my *chai* until the sugar drowns,
then sip the ache of wanting less & less!

This will do, I tell the void's sharp cough,
as rain begins its plain, unasked-for song -
a roof, a chair, a heartbeat's modest work.
The world is loud with more;
I shut the door!!!

The Unspoken Biography of a Wallet

The leather folds lie flat upon my palm,
Each crease a chapter etched by passing years.
At first, it held the weight of possibility -
A single bill, a number hastily
Inscribed on paper thin as summer hopes,
A student ID, bright with promise still.

Then ticket stubs began their quiet collection,
Like fallen petals marking seasons' turns:
The midnight shows, the concerts bleeding dawn,
That coffee shop where love first found its voice
In receipts now faded, tucked between
The wallet's aging ribs, their stories kept.

Success arrived in plastic, gleaming new -
Gold cards & platinum, tokens of a worth
Measured in limits stretching past the stars,
While business cards piled thick as autumn leaves.
The leather stretched to hold ambition's heft,

Each slot a vessel for a dream unfurled.

Her photo came to rest behind clear panes,
Then children's faces multiplied like joy -
School portraits marking time in steady frames,
Each smile a mirror of the years in flight.
The wallet swelled with life's accruing weight,
Too full at times to close against its wealth.

But time makes trades we never quite intend:
Insurance cards replace the movie stubs,
Prescriptions crowd where concert tickets lived,
Appointments fill the spaces party nights
Once claimed. The medications list grows long,
While memories of dancing shorten, dim.

Yet in one pocket, worn to softness now,
That first photograph refuses still to fade -
Two younger souls who thought the wallet light,
Not knowing how its heft would chart their path
Thru' years of gathering & letting go,
Until the leather learned to hold just this:

Enough for now, for one, for quieter days
That ask for less but somehow carry more
In every crease & corner, every fold
That tells our story better than our words -

How life distils itself to essence pure,
In this small archive carried next the heart!!!

The Shrinking Shopping Bag

Mornings witness my gaze, over filter *kaapi's* steam,
Across the park where lives pulse on worn pathways,
In rhythmic steps, in breaths drawn deep & long,
The joggers' dance, the walkers' patient trudge!

Among them drifts a figure, bent by time,
Mr. Kay, with shoulders stooped & slow stride,
His hands clutch a bag, transparent, light,
That swings with quiet resignation - small,
So small now, it barely holds a day's need!

Once, it swelled with promise, brimming full,
When love was young & life's shelves overflowed,
With laughter echoing in crowded rooms,
And plans stretched wide as future's open door!

Then came the growing years, the bursting bags,
The weight of children's hunger & their dreams,
Of schoolbooks, toys & festive feasts prepared,
The market trips of hurried, busy days,

Two hands clasped tight on overstuffed handles!

But seasons change, as do the bags we hold,
Progeny flown on winds of their own worlds,
His hands now lighter, his errands few,
No longer hauling wishes not his own,
No lists that stretch beyond his shrinking needs!

His steps are slower now, his bag much less,
A few beans, a tomato, an onion small,
A sprig of coriander, just enough,
To flavour solitude, to taste the day,
To feed a heart grown quiet, lived enough!

The shrinking shopping bag tells life's own tale,
Of fullness followed by gentle release,
Of holding on & learning to let go,
To carry just enough - no more, no less,
To find contentment in what still remains!

And as he walks, his shadow stretching long,
I sip my *kaapi*, feeling time's own weight,
Watching the arc of life unfold below,
In quiet steps & one small, shrinking bag!!!

It Will Be Better Tomorrow

Keep your chin up, my dearest,
I see the weight you carry, the shadows that linger,
But remember, the sun always knows its way back.

Faith isn't easy - it's stubborn & shy,
But it's there, hiding in the cracks of your resolve,
Waiting to rise like a tide when you least expect it.

You don't have to be unyielding;
Strength isn't in enduring everything.
It's in knowing when to let go,
To say: ***Enough.***

If it feels too heavy, step away.
Leave the storm behind;
Don't let her - or him - or anyone -
Have the power to tilt the axis of your peace.

Some days feel endless,
Like they've stolen the light from your spirit,

But even the longest night
Must eventually bow to dawn.

Tight, tight hugs surround you now,
A fortress of love,
And this promise:

It will be better tomorrow!!!

It Is Okay to Miss Him

The silence spreads where once your laughter dwelled,
A void that echoes thru' the empty rooms,
Consuming spaces once alive with warmth-
The subtle rhythms of a cherished bond.
Your absence carves a landscape strange & cold,
Where memory's soft whispers linger still,
And every corner holds a fragment soft
Of conversations shared, of wisdom pure!

I trace the contours of your gentle touch,
The steady hands that guided & consoled,
The knowing glance that spoke beyond mere words,
A language built of understanding deep.
No platitude can fill this hollow space,
No ritual of grief can mend this tear
That splits the fabric of our shared today
From all the yesterdays we treasured once!

Yet in this pain, a tender truth resides:
To miss you is to honour how you lived,

To feel the depth of love that does not end
When breath departs & physical form fades.
Your spirit dances in the quiet now,
Inhabiting the spaces of our hearts,
A luminous & undismissed presence
That time cannot erode, nor sorrow dim!

So, let the tears flow freely, unashamed-
Each droplet holds a memory, a smile,
A fragment of the legacy you built,
The love that ripples far beyond this moment.
We miss you, yes - and in that missing lies
The truest testament to who you were:
Beloved, cherished, deeply understood,
A light that continues to illuminate!!!

’Twas Always You

The real love story was not found in them,
But in your steps along the quiet path,
Where shadows fell & you began to see
Thru' eyes unclouded by another’s lens,
And carved out joy beneath the weight of doubt!

'Twas the way you softened to your flaws,
Forgiving wounds you thought would never heal,
And held your heart with tenderness & grace,
A sanctuary built from your own hands -
A love that bloomed from roots you’d long ignored!

For what you sought outside had always dwelled
Within the chambers of your open soul.
To love yourself, in wholeness, as you are -
That was the journey written in the stars!!!

Zidd: The Unyielding Will

In silent dawn,
when muscles ache & strain,
A whisper rises from the depths within.
It speaks of fire,
of dreams yet unfulfilled,
Of mountains scaled & chasms overcome.
This voice, this force - in India,
we call it *Zidd.*

It dwells in hearts
of those who dare to reach
Beyond the boundaries of flesh & bone.
When javelin soars
or feet pound dusty tracks,
When sweat & tears blur vision,
Zidd remains
A compass pointing true to glory's peak.

Not mere ambition,
nor simple stubbornness,

But something deeper,
etched in sinew's core.
A refusal to succumb,
to bend,
to break,
When all seems lost
& victory far removed.
Zidd says,
"*Stand tall.*
Your journey's not complete"

From humble villages
to world's grand stage,
This spirit lifts the fallen,
spurs the weak.
It fuels the countless hours
of thankless toil,
The lonely struggles
far from cheering crowds.
In every triumph,
Zidd stands proudly there.

So let the world behold
this force unleashed,
In champions who carry nations' hopes.
For in their eyes burns bright
that ageless flame,

The indomitable will
that India knows as *Zidd.*
Forever pushing limits,
Forging paths anew!!!

I Won't Walk Away!

I won't walk away, though skies may turn to ash,
and clouds sink heavy, burdened with the weight
of years & fears I never meant to bear.
The world has teeth; it chews & spits out dreams,
and yet I plant my feet, an anchor cast.

To walk away is easy in the light,
when mornings crack with laughter on the wind
and all the roads feel soft beneath my step.
But what is joy, if not the child of grit?
To hold my ground when comfort bids me leave.

I've danced with sorrow, drunk its bitter glass,
yet found in every bruise a chance to heal,
to press my hand against the darkest wounds
and tell myself: *not all of life is pain.*
A truth more fierce than joy & twice as rare.

I will not turn my back on what is hard,
for in the struggle, something sacred grows,

a tender root that twists thru' rock & drought,
the stubborn pulse that claims: **I am alive!**
It's not a call to conquer every storm,
but to refuse defeat as life unfolds.

I'll stand, unshaken by the harshest winds,
and let their fury carve me into shape,
for there are paths only the broken know,
where light descends thru' cracks the bold have made.
I won't walk away. This ground is mine to keep!!!

lemme live just a lil more...

lemme live just a lil more...
to taste the bitterness of regret on my tongue,
lemme live just a lil more...
and feel the warmth of joy embrace my soul.
lemme live just a lil more...
to stumble, fall & rise above my failures,
lemme live just a lil more...
to seek the love I thought forever lost.
lemme live just a lil more...
unearth a talent hidden deep within,
lemme live just a lil more...
explore the depths of passions yet unknown.
lemme live just a lil more...
to paint the canvas of my days with vigour,
lemme live just a lil more...
and dance to rhythms I've never dared before.
lemme live just a lil more...
to laugh until my sides ache with delight,
lemme live just a lil more...
and cry the tears that cleanse my weary heart.

lemme live just a lil more...
to touch the stars & feel the ocean's roar,
lemme live just a lil more...
for in this fleeting life, I yearn for more!!!

My Question

I find no common ground
to mix, to talk, to interpenetrate
They are so different. No! Indifferent
to my opinion, any originality
other than their own.
'*We are there to think &*
you to do the bidding' is all I get.
Why this to one who only wants to help?
I do not arrogate to myself
all the wisdom of the world;
I only get by with whatever
I could do for my fellows,
besides my own little things.
But when they are in a spot
they hum & haw over things
past their comprehension.
There then do I perform
the **Rescue Act**.
But why shan't they have me forewarn

them & pre-empt their predicament.
Tell me, tell me, Muse! ***Tell me?***

The Eternal Another

Another scroll, another swipe,
Another FOMO-fuelled hype.
Another show to binge tonight,
Another "*just one more*" despite
The clock that ticks past 2 AM,
Another "*five mins*" (*ad infinitum*).
Another tab of shoes to browse,
Another cart we won't quite rouse
To checkout - but it feels so nice,
Another dopamine paradise.
Another goal post shifting right,
Another "*nearly there*" in sight.
Another square of chocolate broken,
"**Last one**!" - perpetually spoken.
Another deadline we'll outrun,
Another race that's never won.
Another gadget we must own,
Another upgrade yet unknown.
Another status we pursue,
Another view we must review.

Another peak when we arrive,
Reveals another mountain's drive.
Another summit calls our name,
Another height to stake our claim.
Another dream, another scheme,
Another perfect life to gleam.
While Nature's creatures rest content,
We're cursed with endless "***just one more***" intent.
Yet in this chase of endless more,
Perhaps there's something worth fighting for:
Another chance to grow & learn,
Another wisdom yet to earn.
For in our wanting's endless game,
We've built & dreamed & staked our claim.
So here's to us, with boundless hearts,
Still reaching for what lies beyond the stars!!!

Seasons in Motion

The leaves are changing, a slow-motion dance,
Their gradual shift, a gentle velocity.
What is, is - yet never stays the same,
A paradox of constant transformation.
Autumn for some, spring for others, you see,
As Earth tilts its face to & from the sun.
We're all just spinning, at different paces,
Our personal seasons not always aligned.
Love blooms in winter, withers in summer,
Dreams sprout in fall, bear fruit in the spring.
The heart's calendar, a fickle thing indeed,
Rarely syncing with nature's steady beat.
So embrace the flux, the ebb & the flow,
For change is the only constant we know.
In life's grand ballet of perpetual motion,
We're all leaves changing, at our own devotion!!!

Life, the Ultimate Teacher

In seas of time, where tides of change surge high,
Life stands, a sentinel of endless lore.
No classroom walls confine its vast domain,
Nor blackboards hold the wisdom it imparts.

From dawn's first light to dusk's encroaching shade,
Each moment bears a lesson, stark & true.
The Naval Commander's crisp salute at morn,
The civilian's gentle nod - both teachers here.

In triumphs grand & failures' bitter sting,
Life writes its curriculum, bold & clear.
No textbook holds the depths of joy & pain
That forge the soul in life's unyielding forge.

Friends, foes & strangers - all are mentors masked,
Their actions etching truths upon our hearts.
The child's laughter & the elder's sigh
Echo with knowledge time cannot erase.

So, let us raise a toast to life, our guide,
Whose lessons stretch beyond all mortal bounds.
In every breath, a chance to learn anew,
In every step, a classroom without end!!!

You Never Lose Your Way Down the Memory Lane

Shards of yesterday
scattered across the mind's landscape

Broken mirrors
reflecting
distorted truths

We stumble
thru' the labyrinth of recollection
never truly lost

Snapshots of joy
fleeting sorrows
moments suspended in time's amber

Disjointed narratives
weave a fabric of who we are

No map

No compass
Yet we navigate
with unwavering certainty

In the haze of memory
clarity emerges

Fractured & whole
simultaneously

We wander
thru' the maze of our past
always
finding our way home!!!

Why Not Trust Your Intuition?

That quiet voice,
oft drowned by reason's roar -
Why silence what we know
in heart is true?
We seek advice from those
who cannot know
The depths of our desires,
our hidden dreams!

How many chances slip thru'
doubtful hands,
As we debate
the whispers from within?
The path less travelled beckons,
clear & bright,
Yet still we pause,
too fearful to begin.

Trust that small voice,

it knows far more than all
The logic world can offer.
It is you!!!

Unspent Moments

I hoarded time
like coins in pockets deep,
Believing leisure days
would come to spend
These precious moments,
saved with zealous care.
But life, a tattered garment,
frayed & worn,
required constant mending,
and the joy
I'd tucked away
slipped thru' my fingers. . .
lost!

When finally I paused
to count my wealth,
The purse lay empty,
memory's coffers bare.
Beside still waters,
seeking my reflection,

I found a stranger
gazing back at me -
Silver-crowned,
time-etched,
a face unknown,
Yet mine. . .
the cost of moments left unspent.

O, seize the day!
For life's swift current flows,
And waits for no one's leisure
or repose!!!

Roads Written in Smoke

I smell the road unfurling like smoke -
bitter at first, then sweet with possibility,
earth & stone dissolving on my tongue.
The path's aroma shifts with each breath:
pine-sharp ascents, hollow valleys of moss,
the mineral tang of rivers not yet crossed.

My fingers press against the contours of going,
journey a texture rough then smooth in my palms.
I touch distance - it trembles like silk,
catch time between thumb & forefinger,
roll it until it thins to transparency.
The weight of arrival sits heavy in my hands!

Destination is a fragrance that changes
with each step not taken.
I inhale deeply, drawing maps of scent
into my lungs while my skin
reads the terrain's intention,
each pore absorbing the narrative of elsewhere.

My body translates absence into presence.

What eyes miss, nostrils interpret.
What feet avoid, fingertips understand.
The universe rewritten thru' inverted senses -
I am touching what cannot be held,
breathing what cannot be seen,
becoming the road that becomes me!!!

She Used to Live Here

She used to live here - third floor, second window,
the one with the geranium that always tilted left,
as if leaning out to gossip with passersby.
I pass by sometimes, not to linger -
just to confirm the pavement still remembers my shoes!

Her laugh used to bounce off these bricks,
ricocheting into my ribs like an unlicensed firecracker.
Now the building's quieter,
as if holding its breath,
or maybe judging me for the mismatched socks!

She used to live here -
and so did the pizza guy who knew our order by heart,
the neighbour who practiced the keyboard at midnight,
and that pigeon - *Dara* - who stared thru' the window
like he knew all our secrets!

I half expect her to pop-out the door -
hair half-dry, *kaapi* in hand,

offering unsolicited advice about my shirt choices.
But the door stays closed,
and *Dara*, the pigeon, now runs the block!

She used to live here & the air still holds
the faint aftertaste of inside jokes & burnt toast.
I keep walking,
'coz nostalgia is a sneaky little pickpocket -
and I've only got so much heart to spare!!!

simmer

she has become a gentler version of herself...
while her essence remains the same,
time has softened the edges,
allowing depth & richness to surface!

her strength is not in the rush of a roaring flame,
but in the quiet persistence of a steady heat,
where layers of complexity unfold
and the hidden flavours of her soul rise to meet the world!

she has learned the art of patience,
knowing that some transformations
are not meant to be hurried!

her truth is her subtlety,
her pace, deliberate,
her heart, unhurried,
her journey, profound.
SHE is a master of slow, deliberate magic!!!

I Missed You. . .

I missed you quietly, beneath the dusk,
Where shadows stretched like echoes of your name.
No thundered cry, no wail to pierce the night -
Just hollow breaths that vanished into air.
I missed you in the hush of morning rain,
Each drop a whispered thought I left unsaid.
The *chai* cooled beside an empty chair,
And silence stirred where laughter used to live.

I missed you in the pause between my steps,
The fleeting glance at places we had been.
Your absence wove a thread thru' every day,
A gentle pull that tethered me to loss.
I missed you when the world forgot to pause,
While others rushed thru' moments I held still.
I carried you in fragments thru' the hours,
A secret weight that time could not unbind.

I missed you quietly, but still you stayed -
A shadow soft against my aching heart.

Though silence holds the space where you should be,
Your memory still whispers, "**I am here!**"

Bone-Deep

The first cut is never the deepest -
it's the after, the slow bleed
of a name unspoken in the throat,
a rib removed in sleep,
the hollow where a child's hand
once curled like a question mark!

Ask the moth why it flies
into the candle's yes.
Sacrifice is the seed splitting its shell -
subtract the self,
carry the ghost of what might have been!

We burn what we cannot keep:
youth in the kiln of time,
grief in the belly of prayer.
The altar is the space
between two breaths -
a lung's eclipse,
where you whisper this, not me

& the stars dim -
just enough for dawn!!!

Where Light Breaks Thru'

I run, lungs filling with the heavy air,
the weight of morning pressing on my chest.
Yet here, between the trees, the light spills down,
long fingers parting mist & dust alike -
- crepuscular & careless in their grace!

The sun fights thru' the thick & tainted veil,
its beams refracted, fractured, yet alive.
Pollution makes a canvas of the sky,
turns ruin into fleeting art. And so -
I stop. I never stop. But now, I do!

A contradiction standing still mid-stride,
a breathless pause inside a breathless world.
I raise my lens, my witness to the glow -
to irony, to beauty, to decay.
Then, just as swift, the moment folds away!

The run resumes, the road pulls time along,

but somewhere in my mind, the light remains -
not pure, not clean, not perfect - but still there!!!

Nature, Sweet Nature

I stood in awe of what I espied,
Nature was wreathed in a splendour ethereal,
Beauty unrivalled, a fantastic kaleidoscope,
The hills rising one over the other.
A limpid stream threading its way
Thru' the crannies & crevices,
Trees nestling in battle array as it were.
Whistling wind rendering cool the landscape
Oh! what a glorious morn!
I seem to see nature wearing a smile
I stood in the midst of it all
Bewitched, Bewildered & Besotted.
Nothing mattered to me
Save that I was a part of it
And must become one with it....

From Earth's Womb

I am earth's flesh, humble & brown,
Ancient memories of weathered stone,
Ground down by time's patient hand
Into particles of possibility.
Once, I was but scattered sand,
Formless, without purpose or plan,
Until those knowing fingers found me,
Gathered my body from the land!

Water blessed my dusty form,
And I became supple, willing -
A universe of potential,
Spinning on the sacred wheel!

Feel how I yield to pressure,
How I rise beneath skilled palms
That see in my mundane substance
Vessels of grace yet unborn.
I am transformed thru' trust,
Surrendering to the potter's dream.

Each gentle push, each loving curve
Awakens beauty from my being!

Thru' fire's crucible I pass,
From soft earth to lasting art.
What was common becomes precious,
What was shapeless finds its heart!

Now I cradle morning coffee,
Hold flowers reaching toward the sun,
Bear witness to family dinners,
Preserve sacred ashes of the departed,
Keep ancient stories in my glaze.
I am vessel, a bearer of life,
A testament to transformation's power -
Proof that even common earth can rise
To touch the divine thru' human hands.

In my finished form, I remember:
I am still that humble clay,
But now I sing of possibilities
In the language of shape & form.
For in the end, it's not the firing,
Nor the glaze that makes me whole -
It's the vision that saw worth
In simple soil, waiting to be more!!!

What Am I Doing Here?

The horizon stretches endlessly,
a line that promises & mocks in equal measure.
I stand on the deck,
the steel beneath my feet worn smooth by journeys I no longer remember.
The sea, vast & unbothered,
does not care for my questions!

I asked the stars once - they only blinked,
like a signal I was too dense to decipher.
I asked the wind,
but it laughed, slipping past my ears,
its secrets too ancient for my mortal understanding!

What am I doing here?
Is it to sail? To drift?
To catalogue the colour of every sunset,
or to find meaning in the waves
that crash & recede without reason?

Perhaps I am the ship,
not the Captain -
a vessel moved by forces unseen,
directionless yet always moving!

Or maybe I am the anchor,
dragging along the ocean floor,
leaving scars in the sand,
grasping for something solid
in a world that refuses to stay still.

The sea does not answer.
It only moves, eternal & indifferent,
and I remain here,
both questioning & knowing
that no answer will ever be enough!!

Possibility

Each morning, the sun stretches across my face,
a gentle nudge, a whisper: "*Here we go again*"
The kettle hums, steam rises in curls,
transforming water into comfort,
the first of many miracles I won't notice!

My neighbour's child learns to ride her bike,
falls seven times but rises eight, her scraped knees
collecting stories of persistence. Her mother
watches from the porch, remembering perhaps
her own first wobbling journey toward balance!

In the crack of my garden wall, a *gulmohar*
pushes thru' concrete, defying architecture
with nothing but sunlight & stubbornness.
Who taught it such rebellion? The same force
that mends bones, that heals hearts, that whispers
"**maybe**" when all evidence screams "**never**!"

I watch the evening news, its litany of sorrows

threatening to drown hope's quiet pulse, yet
in between disasters, there are always hands
reaching out to strangers, voices rising in song
above the rubble, seeds being planted in war zones!

At night, my son asks about tomorrow.
I could speak of uncertainty, of darkness gathering
at the edges of our world, but instead I tell him
about the moon's faithful return, about seeds
sleeping beneath winter soil, about how every ending
carries within it the seeds of beginning!

For what is possibility but the defiance
of what is, in favour of what could be?
It lives in morning coffee, in Band-Aids on knees,
in the space between heartbeats, in the pause
before "**yes**." It is the bridge we build
between now & next, between fear & faith,
each step a choice to believe in dawn's return!

Even as I write these words, somewhere
a patient opens their eyes after surgery,
a refugee child tastes safety's first sweet breath,
a scientist's failed experiment reveals
an unexpected door. Always, always,
possibility waits in the wings of disaster,
patient as sunrise, persistent as hope!!!

The Admiral's Rations

The Admiral stirs his coffee, a spoon of iron resolve,
To forge his daring path anew, thru' '**standard protocol**'
"*Today, we'll rewrite the playbook*!" he bellows from the deck,
But with one eye on the handbook, lest a comma's moved or pecked!

"*Let's step outside our comfort zone, sailors, sail a different road*!"
But make sure every step you take complies with The Naval Code.
They'll holler "*Bend the rules, Cadets*!" from rigid, uptight spines,
Then push that envelope precisely till it falls within the lines!

Off the beaten path they go, but GPSes in their hand,
Because sailing to safety is still the policy's FIRST command.
And when they're done with rebel talk, they'll strike a

pose so bold,
In pristine-pressed white attire, ironed straight in
standard issue mould!!!

Never stop listening to that small voice

From Mumbai's shores to distant foreign ports,
The oceans taught me more than books could tell.
Command & duty shaped my youthful thoughts,
Yet still that voice within had tales to spell.

When brass & stars no longer graced my shoulders,
I turned to circuits, codes & silicon dreams.
The voice whispered, "*There's more beyond these folders*"
So into business realms, I charted new schemes.

Entrepreneurship called, a siren's song,
I answered, built & watched my visions grow.
Yet when it faltered, that voice grew strong:
"*Your lessons learned have seeds of truth to sow*"

In hallowed halls where minds are shaped & moulded,
I found my place, a mentor's role to fill.
My tales & trials, in lectures now unfolded,
That inner voice now resonates at will.

Thru' hospitals & sickbeds, pain-filled nights,
When body failed & spirit ebbed so low,
That voice remained, a beacon in the fights:
"*Press on, old salt, there's still more life to know*"

Reversals came like waves upon the shore,
Each threatening to erode my hard-won peace.
But anchored deep, that voice evermore:
" ***Your story's far from over, do not cease***"

So here I stand, a mélange of years,
Of Navy blue, of business, & of verse.
That small voice guided thru' my hopes & fears,
A compass true, for better & for worse.

To those who listen, young or worn by time,
I offer this, distilled so one may thrive:
Heed well that voice, your inner paradigm,
It is the surest helm to steer your life!!!

Eighteen Again: A Fool's Manifesto

Oh, sweet eighteen, that golden age of folly,
When consequences seem but distant myths.
I'd gladly trade my wisdom for a chance
To royally screw up my life anew.
This time, I'd double down on every vice,
Embrace each bad decision with a grin.
I'd major in underwater basket weaving,
And minor in interpretative dance.
My savings? Ha! I'd blow them all on schemes
To breed designer pigeons for the rich.
I'd start a boy band called "**The Midlife Crisis**,"
Our hit song: "*Mom's Basement* (Is Where I Belong)."
I'd get a face tattoo of Nicolas Cage,
And pierce my tongue with rusty paperclips.
I'd pick a fight with every bouncer in town,
Then wonder why I wake up in the gutter.
Yes, eighteen me would be a glorious mess,
A cautionary tale, a human train wreck.

For what's the point of youth if not to squander?
To hell with sense, let's make some epic blunders!!!

Requiem to the Uncompleted Task

Oh, task unfinished, line uncrossed, you haunt my list, a lingering ghost.
A constant murmur, a nagging plea, a whispered promise, yet to be!

You hold the seed of what could be, a path untrodden, wild & free.
A canvas blank, a song unsung, a future waiting, to be sprung!

You chide me not with stern reproach, but whisper tales of what I'd approach.
A world of "*maybes*," dreams unseen, a hidden garden, lush & green!

You break the chains of rigid plan, a gentle nudge to be a human.
To chase the whim, the fleeting spark & leave the perfect path in the dark!

For in your incompleteness lies, a world of wonder in disguise.
A chance to learn, to veer, to grow, a seed of chaos, helping me flow!

So, thank you, friend, for though you tease, you nudge me onward, set me at ease.
A testament that life's a quest, not just a list to be obsessed!

For in the gaps, the spaces wide, my truest self, I may confide.
And though you linger, ever near, your gentle whisper, I hold it dear!!!

The Storm We Summon

Anger - a tempest within,
A torrent of self-inflicted pain
You, the unwitting prey!

Flames lick at your soul,
Scorching bridges, burning dreams.
Whispers of wisdom lost in the roar,
Echoes of calm silenced by the storm!

Anger's first casualty:
The Self, now charred & hollow.
A pyrrhic victory!!!

The Beauty of Humility

A soft, fluffy cloud descends upon the heart
Wrapping it in wonder, awe & gentle grace
The ego's veil is lifted, true self shines apart
Radiant beauty revealed, connection's path embrace
Empathy, compassion, kindness blooms take root
In humility's garden, love's sweet fragrance shoots!

In harmony with life's rhythm, ***humility*** dances free
Graceful steps, a grand ballroom of gratitude to see
Every triumph a team effort, every achievement a test
To the human spirit's beauty, in ***humility*** we find rest
Interconnectedness whispers secrets, pride's weeds
pruned away
In ***humility***'s gentle mist, our true selves come to stay!!!

Horizon's Breath

On the cusp of worlds, I stand
Where sand sings Earth's ancient lullaby
And the horizon exhales stories untold

My fingers caress the sky's silken blue
Sending ripples thru' heaven's canvas
As cloud-wisps melt on my tongue, tasting of stardust

The ocean unfurls its depths before me
A living tome of aquamarine secrets
Where merfolk pirouette & leviathans dream

I inhale the spectrum, a bouquet of light
Tangy orange sun & velvet purple dusk
Mingling with the crisp scent of foaming waves

Here, at the nexus of real & surreal
I am a speck of sand & a cosmic giant
Insignificant yet infinite, alone yet all-encompassing

The boundary blurs between self & scene
As I become the vista, the vista becomes me
A sensory symphony of existence unbound

In this moment, stretched between sea & sky
I am the embodiment of wonder
A solitary figure dancing on eternity's shore!!!

Time Flies: A Pilot's Lament

Time, they say, has wings so swift,
But where's the cockpit for this gift?
I'd love to grab the controls, you see,
And park it firmly at half-past three!

Alas! This pilot's license is fake,
No matter how many tests I take.
The hours zoom by, the days, they soar,
While I'm still looking for the chronological door!

So here's the truth, no need to gloss:
In time's airline, we're all just held
As hostages, on this fleeting trip,
Wishing we could make the moments skip!

But since we can't, let's raise a toast,
To time, that sneaky, winged host.
May our journey be a joyful race,
Even if we can't control its pace!!!

To Walking Alone

The path less travelled, they say,
is paved with solitude.
But solitude, I've learned,
is not always loneliness.
It is a quiet courage,
a steady pace
set by your own heart's drum.
To walk alone is to embrace
the whisper of the wind,
the symphony of your own thoughts
unmuted by conversation.
It is a chance to witness the world
with fresh eyes,
to discover the nuances of existence
often drowned out
by the noise of company.
There is a power in this pilgrimage,
a strength that comes
from carrying the weight
of your own convictions.

It is a journey of self-discovery,
a peeling back of layers
to uncover the truest version
of yourself.
Let the doubts that may arise
be a gentle breeze,
urging you forward.
Let the occasional pangs of loneliness
be a reminder of the strength
you possess within.
For in the quietude of walking alone,
you gather the courage
to forge your own path,
to become a beacon for those who seek the same light.
Walk on, then, with head held high,
for even in solitude,
you are never truly alone!!!

Attachments

We cling to things with might & main,
From childhood toys to love's sweet pain.
Our hearts, like lint on Velcro strips,
Stick fast to mem'ries, jokes & quips.

We're tethered to our phones, it seems,
And anchored to our hopes & dreams.
We're fastened tight to fads & trends,
And bonded to our foes & friends.

But life, that sly & crafty elf,
Detaches us from our old self.
So hold on loose & hold on tight,
For change will come, by day or night!!!

A Love Letter to my Books

My oldest friends, your spines worn thin,
each crease & crack a tale within.
"Peter Pan" holds my childhood dreams,
"Pride & Prejudice" taught love's schemes.
"Mockingbird" stirred justice's fire,
"Lord of the Rings" filled me with desire.

From that first day, adventure called -
you caught me, held me, never stalled.
Thru' every joy, each boyhood fear,
you spoke the words I longed to hear.

Books - my windows to worlds unseen,
each page a path, each line serene.
I soared with dragons, sailed the seas,
heard the wind in ancient trees.

You know my soul, my deepest delight,
a companion steadfast, day or night.
When I'm gone & the shelves gather dust,

know this: **our love was more than just.**

A new reader will find you & then,
your magic will spark to life again.
But part of me stays, in each dog-eared page -
for your words taught my soul to engage!!!

Morning Missive from Mr. Filter Kaapi

Rise & shine, dear Vatsan, it's time to wake,
And savour the rich brew that I will make.
My grounds, deep & bold,
Hold aromas yet untold,
A taste that leaves you craving, for goodness' sake!

I'll craft a cup both strong & bright,
With notes of spice & cocoa to delight.
My warmth will gently sweep
Away the fog of weekend sleep,
Leaving you refreshed, alert, ready to ignite!

So come, dear friend & lemme in,
My fragrance is your day's sweet begin.
I'm *Filter Kaapi*, your morning muse,
Here to inspire & enthuse!!!

Just Like That!!!

The rooster crowed, the *Kaapi* was brewed,
Paranthas flipped high, such a tasty mood,
Autos in chorus, horns go rat-a-tat,
Morning bustle began - ***just like that***!!!
The metro was on time, a miracle at best,
No pushing, no shoving, everyone at rest,
The office was calm, no ppts in combat,
A peaceful workday - ***just like that***!!!
Lunch was a feast of *biryani* & *dal*,
Gulab jamuns gleaming, sweet juicy ball,
Colleagues shared jokes, boredom fell flat,
The stress disappeared - ***just like that***!!!
The rains arrived, with a breezy embrace,
Paper boats sailing, children in a race,
Umbrellas bloomed, a street-side format,
My city transformed - ***just like that***!!!
The evening was vibrant with *samosas* & *chai*,
Neighbours gossiping under the cloudy sky
Cricket on rooftops, a six & a spat,
The day turned to night - ***just like that***!!!

The moon smiled down on a land so grand,
Dreams woven gently, like a magic hand,
Tomorrow's a puzzle, some this, some that,
But today 'twas my Dilli - ***just like that***!!!

The Song of Bygones & Tomorrows

Oh, humans, a curious breed we are,
One foot in the future, one stuck in a scar.
We chase El Dorado, a dream out of reach,
While yesterday's drama still lingers on in each.

Wrinkled & worn, a well-thumbed cliché,
"***Bygones be Bygones***," we all seem to say.
But dredge up that grievance, that slight, or that tear,
And the embers of fury will instantly flare.

We plan & we plot for a future so bright,
Financial freedom, bathed in golden light.
Meal prepping on Sundays, with schedules so tight,
Yet tonight's the third night we're binging on fright.

Flickering phantoms from memories past,
Haunt the meticulously regimented path.
So raise a glass high, to this wonderful plight,
Of future-obsessed beings, stuck firmly in tonight.

We contradict, cavort & endlessly strive,
A symphony of chaos, where none can survive?
Nay, dear reader, in this beautiful mess,
Lies the essence of humanity, I do confess.

For it's this very tension, this push & this pull,
Fuelling innovation, that makes our lives full.
So let's laugh at ourselves, with a whimsical sigh,
And embrace the absurdity, with a tear in our eye!!!

Autobiography of an Unread Book

I'm just a book on the shelf, you see,
With stories & knowledge inside of me,
I long to be read & cherished, it's true,
But alas, my owner has other things to do.

Sometimes he looks at me & smiles,
Proud of his "**great taste**" all the while,
But I can't help but feel a little sad,
For I'm just a decoration, not something he's had.

I long to be taken down & opened up,
To be caressed, page by page, like a pup
But until then, I'll just sit here & wait
On this bookshelf of his, in a dormant state!

So here I sit, collecting daily dust,
A once great story, now covered in rust.
But I hold onto hope, for someday he'll see,

That the real joy is in reading, **not in displaying me**!!!

Autobiography of a Bookworm

I have a confession I need to make,
My obsession with books is no mistake,
I can't resist their alluring pages,
And the escape they provide in stages.
Some people may say I read too much,
But to me, it's a heavenly touch,
A world of imagination & wonder,
Keeps my mind from going under.

My shelves are bursting with books of every kind,
Fiction, non-fiction, you name it, you will find,
Books on science, history & romance,
I can't help but pick them up on chance.
Poem, biographies, all genres I adore,
They take me to places I've never been before,
I laugh, I cry, I learn & I grow,
My love for books - a never-ending flow.

My bank account might sometimes suffer,

As I add more books to my library buffer,
But when I hold books in my hands,
I feel like I've found a treasure in foreign lands.
So, I'll continue to read books with glee,
For there's no other place I'd rather be,
Lost in a world of words, syntax & prose,
My love for books just grows & grows!!!

Autobiography of Sorry

In a world where I found myself often astray,
I lived my days with hesitation's breath.
Not born to grandeur or in gilded halls,
But where humility's soft echo calls to me.
My childhood filled with dreams & wonderings,
Learning the world's intricate patterns slowly.
I stumbled thru' my youth with awkward grace,
A half-formed smile upon my well-meant face.

In school, I was the boy who always tried,
Though Chemistry bewildered my young mind.
Teachers would say, "*He's bright but often lost*"
My thoughts meandering at their own expense.
Love, as they claim, demands a gentle touch,
Yet my heart sighed in quiet moments of shame.
Words I had wished to speak aloud to others
Were swallowed whole by fears, both shy & proud.

In work, I sought to carve myself a name,
Yet found myself unchanged, still searching.

A paper pusher, turning wheels unseen,
While yearning for something of substance.
I've glimpsed, in fleeting moments rare but true,
A better version of myself emerge.
But more often I stumbled, tripped and fell,
My life becoming one long sigh of "**Oh well**"

So now I write this modest testament
From quiet corners of my simple home.
A story not of glory, fame or wealth,
But of a man who tried, despite it all.
For in each sorry moment lies a tale
Of effort, hope & sometimes, yes, failure.
But thru' it all, I still remain myself,
A humble scribe recording my own history!!!

Confessions of a Dictionary Darling [My Ode to the WOTY 2025 (Word of The Year) – Manifest]

Dear fellow words, gather 'round if you please,
(*You thought 'rizz' & 'situationship' would be the tease!*)
But here I am, your **WOTY** supreme,
Making Oxford & Collins lose their steam.
"***Manifest this, manifest that***" - they say all day,
Like I'm some genie granting wishes away!

From TikTok trends to Instagram reels,
I'm **#hashtagged** more than how Gen-Z feels.
Once a humble verb in dictionaries old,
Now I'm meme-worthy, trending & bold.
"**WOTY! WOTY!**" they chant my name,
Like I'm some lexical hall of fame!

Some use me for their vision boards,
Others in their motivational hoards.
"I manifest a million bucks!"
(*Good luck with that - I'm not Starbucks*)
Yet here I stand, crowned & proud,
A WOTY that does vocabulary proud!

P.S. To *'Rizz'* & *'Swiftie'*, better luck next time!
Being WOTY? Well, that's simply manifest divine!!!

The Masala Dabba: From Rasoi to Runway

Saasumaa's *masala dabba*, worn & wise,
Over 3 decades of spices cradled in its heart,
Each compartment holding memories & time -
The *jeera* that danced in morning's tempering,
The *haldi* that stained palms with stories!

But today, I scroll thru' digital bazaars,
Where humble steel now dons a royal cloak:
Behold! The *masala dabba* reimagined -
Swarovski crystals & Kashmiri craft,
Peacock feathers etched in shimmering brass,
A miniature palace for cumin & clove -
A touch of bling for the heart of the *rasoi*!

"**5000 rupees!**" my great-grand *Bua* would cry,
"*For what? To hold the same old jeera seeds?
Did dhania powder learn to spin pure gold?
Does ajwain now come blessed by temple priests?*"
The marketing gurus nod & simply say:

"Tradition meets luxury, Ma'am. That's the way!"

No longer content with mere utility,
These *dabbas* gleam with artisanal ambition -
Rosewood rims, brass clasps, velvet-lined grace,
As if cumin deserved a throne of gold!

And yet, in this age of curated kitchens,
Where even coriander must pose for Insta likes,
I hear whispers from seasoned wrists of old,
Scoffing at ornamental impostors -
For their *dabbas* hold stories, not hashtags!

Still, somewhere in a *rasoi* quietly hums
The true heart of the kitchen - old & plain,
Unseen by algorithms, but essential:
A simple round box, rich with memory -
The sun around which every *curry, tadka & chai*
revolves!

Whether bejewelled or weathered with age,
The *masala dabba* remains what it's always been:
The heart of every Indian kitchen's soul -
Holding close the spices that flavour life,
One humble spoonful at a time!!!

Mental Pajamas & Witty Rapiers

They call it "**attitude**" - that superior air,
But I just won't settle for conversation so bare.
Small talk of weather & Gandhian dramas?
No thanks, I require some mental pajamas!

It's not being cocky, it's wanting some spice!
Bland chit-chat feels like a dull literary vice.
They see a raised brow & cry "**What a snob!**"
I just crave rapiers that wittily jab!

Don't mistake my standards for mere attitude,
If talk was nutrition, I'd be badly skewed.
I want witty banter that opens mind's doors,
Not recaps of gamers or insufferable bores!

This disappointment's not attitude, simply fatigue
From comments dull, hollow - a mental hedge siege.
So, don't judge the book by its self-assured cover,
I'm just holding out for my fervid turn-over!

Call me picky or "**extra**" - I own that with pride,
While you drown in gossip, I'm open-mind wide.
Attitude? Nah, I just seek substance & zest.
Save bland for white bread; my appetite's redressed!!!

Semper Gratum (always grateful)

This swift age where screens & time conspire,
We chase the fleeting pulse of pleasure's glow,
Yet, in the quiet breath of morning's calm,
Stillness offers gifts as deep as night.

Not every step must race toward the thrill,
For in the hum of daily, steady hours,
The mundane blooms with grace, a subtle joy.

When did we lose the art of idle peace,
Of watching leaves drift slow upon the breeze?
Semper gratum - let this be our creed,
To cherish every grain of life's slow sands,
To find in boredom's grasp a gentle hand,
And learn that even in the quiet's fold,
A life well-lived embraces time's slow gold!!!

silence speaks

mea culpa, my burden to bear,
in quietude, I stand still -
bound by remorse, a shadowed truth.

the heart whispers,
its confessions etched in time,
in the stillness of night,
the quiet holds the weight of words unspoken,
a silent prayer for forgiveness, unyielding.

mea culpa - my spirit bends,
under the weight of silence,
nishabdam echoes in the hollow,
where the soul finds no solace.

in stillness,
two worlds converge,
a dance of guilt & grace!!!

Leap or Linger

Familiar walls, a cozy prison.
Stagnant dreams!

Fear whispers, "***Stay***"
Growth beckons beyond.
The unknown terrifies & tempts.

Will you leap?
Or remain ensnared?

The Thrill of Watching Paint Dry

Behold! The grand spectacle of pigment's slow demise,
As molecules of colour cling to walls with grim resolve.
O, how the heart races at each microscopic shift,
While time, that fickle jester, tiptoes by on muffled feet.
The universe contracts to this: a patch of beige on white,
A battle 'twixt wetness & the creeping touch of air.
What epic tales are told in each laborious drip?
What cosmic truths revealed in bubbles' fleeting lives?
Excitement builds! A speck of dust alights upon the scene,
Adding drama to this sluggish saga of the brush.
The coffee grows cold, forgotten in this riveting display,
As eyelids flutter, heavy with the weight of pure suspense
Monotony, sweet siren, sings her lullaby of blah,
While ennui dances slowest waltz across the barren mind.
Yet lo! A revelation dawns with each successive coat:
In boredom's crafty clutches, we find thrills anew.

So let us raise a toast to paint, that viscous harbinger,
Of dreams deferred & afternoons that stretch to infinity.
For in its gradual conquest of blank space, we glimpse
The truest art of all: **the masterpiece of tedium!!!**

When is the Vacation from Schadenfreude Gonna Be Over?

Oh joy! Another disaster is in sight,
Time to forward it left & right.
Your eyes are gleaming, fingers twitching,
To spread misery, ain't that bewitching?

Click, share, repeat - your daily *mantra*,
No check needed, you're no doubter.
"***Look how awful!***" you proclaim with glee,
As if bad news is your daily cuppa tea!

Your head's so deep in your own rear view,
You've lost all sight of what's really true.
Stuck in an echo chamber, nice & snug,
As if reality's some kinda harmful drug!

Doom-scrolling champion, misery's friend,
When will this "**hobby**" of yours ever end?

Do you ever tire of this grim delight?
Or is spreading gloom your sole appetite?

Headlines scream, your heart's a-flutter,
"***Our country's doomed!***" you eagerly mutter.
Never mind context, who needs the whole story?
When half-truths can paint all in such gory?

You're so busy shovelling all this crap,
You can't see you're drowning in your own trap.
Wallowing in muck, you think you're so wise,
But you're just peddling propaganda & lies.

So tell me, my dear purveyor of woe,
When will your schadenfreude vacation go?
Or is this permanent residence you've chosen?
In a world where empathy remains frozen?

Perhaps one day you'll extract your head,
From where the sun don't shine, as it's said.
And share some news that actually matters,
Not just junk that depresses & shatters!!!

O Machine, Can You Dream?

With circuits humming, lines of code entwine,
An "**Intelligent**" machine, a grand design.
Yet wisdom's essence, it cannot embody,
For life's rich canvas defies mere applied study.
Can algorithms grasp a mother's warm embrace?
Or capture the sublime in a lily's transient grace?
What of courage's fire, when fears must be braved?
Such nuanced humanity remains undigitised, unsaved.
Patriotism's fierce pride in the colours unfurled,
Brotherly bonds forged in this crazy world,
The soul's still silence, a wave's mighty roar,
These are the songs no CPU has yet learned to score.
So call it "**Artificial Capability**" at best,
For true intelligence requires a living test.
A computational mind, however bright,
Cannot experience being's profound light.
A paradox it is, this "**Intelligent**" device,
Clever gears constrained, can't break life's profound Vice.
Let us find new words for these amazing feats,

Lest we speak oxymorons when "**Intelligence**" we repeat!!!

Denial

I am not in denial.
I'm just... strategically postponing reality,
like a toddler hiding behind a curtain,
convinced the world disappears if they can't see it.

Bills? What bills?
Those are *future me's* problem -
that guy's a sucker anyway.

The scale must be broken.
I didn't eat that entire pizza;
half of it evaporated.
Thermodynamics, probably.

My inbox isn't overflowing,
it's just...*abundantly populated* -
a thriving digital ecosystem.
Who am I to disrupt biodiversity?

The mirror is lying again,

reflecting some older, wearier imposter.
I'm *practically immortal*,
fuelled by *kaapi*, denial & sheer audacity.

The car doesn't need gas,
it's running on *optimism* & the fumes of my delusions.
The check engine light is merely a suggestion.

Love isn't over -
we're just on an extended *mutual misunderstanding*.
They'll come around.
Or orbit back.
Planets do that.

I'm fine. Really.
Totally fine.
(If I say it three times fast, it becomes true, right?)

Denial isn't a river in Egypt -
it's a five-star resort,
and I'm lounging by the pool,
sipping a cocktail called **Blissful Ignorance!!!**

Care to join me?

tossed

she is a whirlwind of energy,
flung into the heat of the moment,
her ingredients a kaleidoscope
of bold choices, unexpected twists,
and a pinch of madness!

her essence sizzles in the hot wok of life,
where oil, sauces & spices
collide in chaotic harmony,
turning raw edges into something vibrant,
her imperfections coated with flavour!

she is never still -
each toss reveals a new facet of her being,
and with every flip, she becomes
more balanced, more complex, more her!

finished with a flourish,
garnished with grace,

she is the dish that lingers -
unforgettable, full of life & **utterly her own!!!**

Stirred & Yet Not Shaken [Stirred From Sleep; Shaken By Quake]

At dawn, the earth grumbled beneath the city,
a growl deep-throated, ancient in its bones,
plates grinding like forgotten grievances,
shifting the stories stacked upon its skin.
Walls shivered. Sleep tumbled from startled eyes.
The ground beneath, once certain, swayed & sighed,
a carpet pulled by unseen, steady hands!

In the kitchen, I stood still, watching water
turn to steam, rising against tremors' touch.
Fingers measured out tea leaves, a ritual
of rhythm & calm amidst the shaking.
Masala's spice waltzed with ginger's warmth,
cardamom whispered of familiar comforts,
while milk curled into amber's embrace!

My son sat, his eyes half-mooned with fatigue,

today's equations weighing on his brow,
numbers rigid in their ordered balance,
untouched by the shifting ground below us.
I poured the *chai* with hands that held the cup
a little longer, a little tighter too,
as if to steady more than just the brew!

He took the cup, both hands cradling heat,
his shoulders easing under its familiar weight,
a comfort learned young, from generations past -
how warmth wraps around a body & stays,
how the world may quake but *chai* remains still,
a fragrant anchor in the tempest's eye!

I watched him drink, each sip a small defiance,
a whisper of permanence against the shift,
for today's final exam loomed large, etched in ink,
questions certain, answers set in stone,
in stark contrast to earth's heaving breath,
which spoke of time's cruel, transient hand!

The house settled. The tremors rolled away,
but I stood there, steeped in the knowing
that plates would grind again, as they must,
that certainties would sway, as they do.
Yet here we stood, sipping against the quake,

held by the warmth of *chai* & love poured deep,
stirred & yet not shaken, by earth or by time!!!

The Ballad of the Infodemic IDIOT

Listen here, ye hypochondriacs bold,
with your laptops & tablets of gold!
You drown in a sea of diagnoses dire,
where every rash spells a funeral pyre!

The internet's vast, a monstrous maze,
filled with quacks & with charlatan's praise.
They peddle their cures with a click & a grin,
while your real ailment just lingers within!

Think you've spotted a tumour, a growth likely benign?
Don't fret o'er those articles, most likely malign!
Those pop-up ads hawking a magical brew,
are snake oil salesmen in a digital hue!

Seek out a doctor, a scholar of health,
not some blogger obsessed with monetary stealth.
Leave the diagnoses to those who have trained,
'ere your web-surfing habits leave you quite drained!!!

Purple Inheritance

Across this field of lavender stars, I see your smile
In each unfurling petal, your spirit in their reach.
Almost three decades gone, yet still you chase that childhood hue,
From painted walls to garden dreams - your purple truth!

The world may wrap you in its monochrome demands,
But daughter, keep this wildflower heart I've watched you grow.
These blossoms, like my love, need no rhyme to speak their depth -
A father's quiet wonder at the woman blooming still!!!

Lies

Lies are a web, silken threads spun,
Deception's intricate design.
Each fibrous strand, a falsehood begun,
Ensnaring truth in its confining line.
Lies may glisten, appealing at first,
Until more lies are woven to uphold.
The more ensnared, the harder to burst
From the fabricated lies you're told.
Yet truth cuts thru with a clarity blessed,
Slicing lies, allowing light to pervade.
The web unravels, finally confessed!!!

Elbow Bending, Couch Indentations & Zomato Biryani (How & Why the Streets of India are gonna be deserted on Sunday)

Silent streets stretch beneath the Sunday sun,
While a billion hearts beat in living rooms.
One nation, one pulse - Dubai's distant drum!

Couches bear witness, cushions compress
Under the weight of hope & history,
New indentations form with each close call!

The elbow bends - a national exercise,
Glasses raised in triumph, or to drown
The sorrow of a wicket tumbling down.

Ice melting like resolve after six hours,
Amber liquid courage for the faint of heart!

Delivery apps crash under finger-taps,
As *biryani* arrives at countless doors,
Forgotten until that crucial over ends.
"**Not now!**" we tell the hapless delivery boy,
Who hurries to the next cricket hostage!

The Black Caps versus Men in Blue,
A battle painted on a billion screens,
While movie halls stand hollow as bone,
Their only patrons those who stream the match!

Somewhere, a senior player's mother prays,
Her son's last dance with this elusive cup.
Somewhere, a child watches wide-eyed,
Tomorrow's hero learning what it means
To carry dreams heavier than willow wood!

The remote - a surgeon's tool we clutch,
To mute advertisements, to rewind that shot,
To pause reality when nerves can't take more!

Work emails wait like spurned lovers,
Monday's problems postponed by mutual consent.
For today we are not doctors, drivers, teachers -

We are the twelfth man, screaming from afar!

So bend that elbow, sink deeper in that couch,
Let Zomato's riders know your door,
For rare is the communion of a nation
United in cricket's sacred liturgy!

The streets can have us back when stumps are drawn,
When history is written, when cups are raised or hopes deferred.
But for now, we vanish from public view,
A disappearing act that happens once in a **Blue**!

For what is a city but people?
And people are elsewhere on Sunday -
Leaning forward, breathing hard, living every ball,
Their footprints temporarily erased from roads,
As Dubai holds India's collective soul!!!

~ A dedication to the Champion's Trophy Finals to be held on Sunday, 09th Mar 2025

Unrequited Love

Unrequited love, a vine ever-climbing,
Grasping for reciprocation's sun.
Tendrils stretching, yearning, miming
The warmth of amorous rays to bask upon.
It scales emotional walls, undeterred,
Seeking chinks where affection may root.
But masonry stays rigid, love unheard,
As the vine's offerings find no pursuit.
Still it persists in verdant desire,
Hopeful that constancy will bring its prize.
Unrequited, it grows,
though love's fire lacks pyre!!!

The Anthem of the Boss (A Corporate Ode to the Grind)

Rise, O workers, the dawn's aglow,
The office awaits; there's no time to slow.
Forget the Sunday, the coffee, the wife,
EBITDA dreams are the very spice of life!

Burnout's a badge; wear it with pride,
Productivity's the chariot you must ride.
Sleep is for mortals, not corporate knights,
Excel warriors conquer all nights!

Why linger at home, staring at walls?
The Boardroom's your temple, answer its calls.
Family dinners? A totally frivolous plight,
Stakeholder smiles are the only true delight!

Competitors grind for 90-hour weeks,
Your 50's a nap, or so wisdom speaks.

The GDP's past; EBITDA's our true flame,
The margins grow; let's play the game!

"*Work smarter, not harder,*" Anand Mahindra said,
But bosses demand your sweat instead.
Forget the *chai*, drop the Netflix queue,
Toil is the mantra - it's all on you!

So sharpen your pencils, your wits, your soul,
Burn bright like coal to achieve the goal.
Let's sing this anthem, with laughter or tears,
To the office grind... for the next 40 damn years!!!

No Right Angles: No Wrong Ones Either (Lessons from Nature)

Look up -
the branches don't follow rules,
twisting, stretching, reaching,
never asking if they're right or wrong.
No symmetry, no blueprint,
just movement, instinct, growth!

And yet -
there is beauty, effortless, undeniable,
in the way they weave their chaos,
cradling the moon like a secret,
framing the sky without ever trying!

Nature doesn't pause to measure,
doesn't hesitate before bending,
doesn't fight the wind -
it moves, it flows, it becomes!

And still, we draw lines,
box ourselves in, straighten, correct, perfect,
as if perfection were something fixed,
as if beauty needed rules!

But the trees laugh, the moon winks,
and the night whispers -
there are no right angles here.
There never needed to be!!!

My Mother

My mother's warmth, a sun's embrace,
Her ever-loving eyes were my go-to place,
A nurturing soul, with tenderest grace!

With patient heart & guiding hands,
She led me thru' life's shifting sands,
Her wisdom echoes, like ocean's bands!

Pillar strong whenever troubles came,
Her faith in me is ever & always the same,
A love unconditional, like the holy flame!!!

Requiem for the Unspoken

You were never a name I memorised,
nor a voice I could recall in the hush of evening.
Yet, you were there - woven into the quiet fabric of my days,
a steady rhythm in the metronome of mornings.

The park bench still stands,
but it no longer holds the weight of your presence.
The dogs sniff the air, puzzled -
where is the hand that once scattered kindness like breadcrumbs?

You moved thru' the world unhurried, yet purposeful,
wrapped in white as if draped in moonlight,
pausing before the sacred tree - not seeking, not asking,
only bowing, as if in quiet communion with time itself!

I never asked your name.
I never spoke your story aloud.
Yet, your absence hums in the spaces you once filled,

a silence that lingers, heavier than words!

Today, the fire will rise,
and the sky will claim what the earth once cradled.
But here, in the echoes of unspoken knowing,
you remain!

Om shanti!!!

in hot water

the accidental alchemist,
dropped into a boiling cauldron of chaos,
edges fraying, essence steeping,
swirling thru' life's unrelenting heat!

unprepared? often.
unrewarded? sometimes.
yet it's here, in the roiling bubbles of risk,
that the art of survival is mastered!

scorched by overconfidence,
burned by bad timing,
& seasoned with a pinch of recklessness -
a recipe for disaster,
or perhaps, brilliance!

for it is in the heat of the moment
that flavour emerges,
grit dissolves into resilience,
& raw potential transforms into

something richer, something stronger,
something undeniably unique!

in hot water,
but always steeped in the lessons
only fire can teach!!!

The Fickle Fate of Being Needed: An Ode to Fair-Weather Friends

When you're useful, they sing your praise,
Your name on their lips for days & days.
But when your purpose has been served,
Their attention, it's quickly swerved.
No more mention, no more thought,
Your existence, so easily forgot.
In times of need, you're their best friend,
But when it's over, the friendship ends.
It's a harsh reality, but oh so true,
People's love is often just a ruse.
They'll keep you close when you're in demand,
But once you're not, they'll let go of your hand.
So don't be fooled by fleeting fame,
Or those who only call your name,
When they need something from you,

For their affection is rarely true.
Instead, cherish those who stay,
Beside you, come what may.
Whose love is steady, come rain or shine,
And whose hearts with yours always entwine!!!

Onto the Next Freebie

In the land of milk & honey, where the nectar flows so free,
Lives a tribe with open palms, shouting, "***What's in it for me?***'
They ride the winds of fortune, with pockets ever bare,
Grabbing at the newest whims, with a greedy, grasping flair.

Oh, give them what they covet, for their need is never small,
A sop here, a freebie there, they must possess them all.
They swipe & snatch with fervour, like children in a store,
But gratitude? It's lost on them; they always want some more.

Their eyes are set on prizes, gleaming bright in gaudy light,
With hearts so cold & hollow, never feeling quite contrite.

They chant their incantations, "***More for me, for I deserve!***"
Entitlement their anthem, they sing it without nerve.

They scorn the working masses, who toil thru' night & day,
For these souls of privilege, it's far easier to sway.
"***Why earn what's freely given?***" they chuckle with a grin,
As they hunt the next big handout, their favourite kind of sin.

Oh, look at them so giddy, at the prospect of a deal,
Their franchise cheaply purchased, their pride an easy steal.
For in their world of plenty, where effort is a curse,
They've lost the sense of value, their souls an empty purse.

But woe to those who question, who dare to call them out,
For they'll be met with scorn & rage, a tantrum & a pout.
"**Unfair!**" they scream, "**Ungrateful!**" as they clamour for the prize,
Blinded by their avarice, that singular truth - a thin disguise.

So here they stand, relentless, in the line for something free,
A congregation of the selfish, lost in their decree.
Onto the next freebie, they march with a greedy pace,
In the annals of entitlement, they've firmly found their place!!!

Palm Lines & Market Tides

The lines on the palm, etched by time & chance,
Whisper secrets of destiny in a cryptic dance.
They tell of paths yet walked,
Of loves found, of fortunes made,
But how much of it is truth & how much is fate?
Are they merely our own projections -
A desperate attempt to impose order on an otherwise
random life?

And then, the indices - the pulse of society's anxiety,
In a frenetic ballet of numbers that rise & fall,
Dictating moods, fortunes & futures.
Are these not the same as the lines on our hands?
A product of human creation - patterns in the chaos,
A desperate attempt to make sense of the vast unknown,
And yet, we place our faith in them!

The market, like the palm, doesn't simply reflect reality -
it creates it.
It's a mirror, distorted & amplified,

Telling us more about who we are than what is.
Riding the waves of stock prices!
We see our own desires, fears, insecurities reflected.
The bull charges forward & we surge with hope;
The bear lurks in the shadows & we recoil in dread.
We let these numbers shape our choices, our lives,
As if the path to happiness could be found in a ticker symbol,
As if peace of mind could be bought or sold!

But perhaps there's something deeper here.
What if the palm, with its lines & the market, with its fluctuations,
Are merely two sides of the same coin?
Both are efforts to predict what we cannot control,
To find patterns in the unpredictable,
To answer that age-old question: What happens next?

We humans are storytellers, after all.
We look for patterns where there are none,
We impose meaning on randomness,
All in an attempt to soothe the anxiety of the unknown.
And when we can't find it in the stars,
Or in the scroll of a palm,
We look to the stock market to give us the answers!

But here's the paradox:

The more we try to control the future,
The less we actually control.
The market behaves like the palm - full of uncertainty,
Always shifting, always uncertain,
Just as life itself is.
And in that uncertainty, we cling to our illusions of control,
Even though we know, deep down,
That the only thing we can truly predict
Is that the future remains forever unwritten,
And we are just actors in its unfolding drama!

So maybe it's not the lines on the palm or the numbers on the screen
That determine our fate.
Maybe it's the way we choose to interpret them -
The meaning we assign to the chaos.
Perhaps we are not bound by the lines,
Nor dictated by the markets,
But are free, instead, to navigate the space in between,
Where possibility resides!

And in the end, the lines on the palm,
The peaks & valleys of the market,
Are just reflections of a deeper truth:
That we are constantly searching,
Constantly interpreting,

Constantly seeking meaning in a world

That offers no easy answers!!!

serein*

whispered sky weeps,
a twilight's tender embrace -
earth drinks in silence!

dew & dusk merge,
soft trails of unspoken love -
night blooms with echoes!

serein lingers,
fragile breath of fading day -
nature's quiet hymn!!!

**light drizzle or mist that falls from a clear sky, often after dusk*

velleity*

whispers arise,
soft trails of unformed yearning -
dreams dissolve in mist!

a quiet ache,
ribbons of tender longing -
untouched, they falter!

velleity flows,
desires too faint to awaken -
gone with the moment!!!

* *an inclination, but not strong enough to lead to action*

The Window

The window stands, a silent sentinel,
a frame for stories etched in glass & light.
Its surface cool, a barrier so thin,
yet vast enough to hold a world of ache.
Here, lovers press their palms against the pane,
their breath a foggy plea to close the gap -
to touch the one who lingers just beyond,
a shadowed figure, almost close enough.

The heart gazes out, not just to find the other,
but to catch a glimpse of its own reflection -
a flicker of the self, half-known, half-dreamed,
a face that shifts with every passing cloud.
It is a mirror, yes, but also more:
a portal where the finite meets the infinite,
where longing stretches toward the horizon's edge,
and the mundane dissolves into the magical.

Thru' it, the world becomes a living canvas -
the golden blush of dawn, the silver rain,

the dance of leaves that whisper secrets old.
It is not just a view, but a vision:
a reminder that there's always more to see,
more to feel, more to love, more to become.
The window holds the ache of what is now,
but also the promise of what might be.

It is the threshold where the soul takes flight,
where yearning meets the vastness of the sky.
A fragile boundary, yet a boundless bridge,
it calls to us, a quiet, constant voice:
"***There is always more. Step closer. Look again***"

84. Compassion

I believe a heart that's kind-hearted & true,
sees the pain & plights others go thru'
And yearns to act, to help renew,
with compassion's touch like morning dew!
Over those whose lives have been stricken by clashes,
or know only days of struggle & tussle
Compassion shines its gentle light,
offering care to ease their plight!

We're ennobled when we ease another's load
and brighten their way on life's difficult road!!!

The Ever-Retreating Tomorrow: A Tragicomic Ode

O glorious Tomorrow! Thou eternal tease,
Where yoga mats lie unopened, pristine still,
And Zumba videos gather digital dust.
Each night I swear upon my mother's name,
"***Kal se pukka***"* - tomorrow, yes, for sure!

The gym membership card smirks from my wallet,
While WhatsApp groups of "**5AM Club Delhi**"
Send perky messages I'll read at noon.
My running shoes, bought during Diwali sales
(*Three pairs in hopeful colours, all unused*),
Judge me silently from their Flipkart box!

The meal prep containers, stackable dreams,
Stand empty like my fitness resolutions,
While Swiggy's notifications mock my plans
Of quinoa bowls & kale smoothies divine.

"*Just one last order*," whispers tonight's biriyani,
"*Tomorrow we'll embrace that salad life!*"

The meditation app, paid premium version,
Sends gentle reminders of mindful peace,
While I doom-scroll thru' reels till 3 AM,
Convinced that dawn will bring enlightenment,
And screenshots of to-do lists multiply
Like promises made to distant relatives!

O Tomorrow! You're like that friend who says
"*Let's catch up soon!*" but never sets a date,
Or like Mom's "***beta, shaadi kab karoge?***"**
Forever asked but never answered true.
You're that divine *idli-sambar* breakfast
I'll wake up early for... but never do!

Yet still we court you, eternally hopeful,
Like cricketers chasing World Cup dreams,
Or uncles forwarding "Good Morning" texts,
Believing that this time will be different,
That you, Tomorrow, won't play hard to get,
That finally we'll catch your fleeting form!

But lo! You're like a mirage in Rajasthan,
Forever dancing just beyond our reach,
While we, eternal optimists supreme,

Keep pushing dreams beyond tonight's sunset,
For surely, SURELY, tomorrow's the day
When all our "***kal karenge***"*** turn to "**NOW**"!

[**Kal se pukka* = Definitely from tomorrow]
[***beta, shaadi kab karoge* = Son/daughter, when will you get married?]
[****kal karenge* = will do it tomorrow]

[In partnership with: The Procrastinator's Society of India (*Meeting scheduled for tomorrow, obviously*)]

The Beauty in Difficulty: Notes to My Children

Unfamiliar paths & difficult roads,
Are not for the faint of heart.
But those who dare to take the plunge,
Find that they play a vital part.
For in these treacherous terrains,
Lies a beauty few have seen.
A world of wonder, mystery & awe,
That only the brave & bold can glean.

So don't be afraid to take the plunge,
To tread where others fear.
For in the end, it's the road less travelled,
That takes you to a place most dear.
And though the journey may be tough,
And the way may seem unclear,
Just keep your head up & your heart strong,
And you'll find the path that's near.

For it's in the challenges we face,

That we find our inner strength.
And it's in the moments of adversity,
That we truly learn to think.
So take that first step into the unknown,
And let your spirit soar.
For the path that's unfamiliar or difficult,
Is the one that takes you to something more!!!

Keys Change Shape, But Never Weight

The first key is light, almost imaginary,
a tiny skeleton of metal & freedom,
turning open a bicycle's rusty promise.
It jingles in my pocket, a song of afternoons
and scraped knees.

Then come the keys that rattle -
lockers filled with crumpled notes & candy wrappers,
a scooter, vibrating with reckless velocity,
a door that sticks in a room too small to dream in,
but mine, still mine.

The keys get heavier.
A chipped apartment key, smelling of paint & possibility,
a car key that smells of late nights & half-believed
directions,
the house key - heavier than it looks,
its teeth sharp enough to cut me into "**home**"

Office keys come sterile & cold,
their weight a quiet negotiation of who I must become
between Nine & Six.
A safe key arrives last,
its turn slow, deliberate - a hinge groaning with
the weight of what I can't afford to lose.

One day, there's a key I can't hold.
It isn't metal. It isn't warm.
It's the echo of every lock I left behind,
and every door that still remembers me!!!

Holi Without You

The colours arrive, loud & laughing,
spilling into streets, into skies, into skin -
and I smile, 'coz how could I not?
It was your festival first, before it ever became mine.

I see you still, in the riot of pinks & blues,
your laughter louder than the clamour of a thousand voices,
your joy untamed, splashed across the world
like it couldn't be contained by one heart alone.

I smile... but the ache knows better.
It reminds me - softly, cruelly -
that you are not here.
Not in the crowd, not in the colour, not beside me.

I want to play, to lose myself in the chaos,
but I fear the colours will only deepen the emptiness,
that each splash will paint a hollow where YOU used to be.

So I stand apart, watching joy unfold without me.
It shouldn't be enough - and yet, somehow, it is.
In their laughter, I hear an echo of yours.
In their wild abandon, I see the light that once danced in
your eyes.

And though my hands remain clean, uncoloured,
my heart wears every hue of you - still, always.
Bittersweet| Melancholic| Beautiful|

Holi belongs to you.
And thru' you, it still touches me!!!

Relationship Ruckus: A Survival Guide

Oh, cruel fate - must you play referee,
In this never-ending emotional Grand Prix?
Where loved ones test my patience & grace,
And drama's a guest who won't leave my place.

Words collide like bumper cars,
Intentions crash, leaving emotional scars.
Relatives, friends - a turbulent crew,
Why must affection feel like a hullabaloo?

But wait - shall I sulk, throw a tantrum, or stew?
Drown in despair like a tragic debut?
Nay, I declare, I shan't be dismayed,
This heart's not a doormat - it's handmade!

For love's a messy, tangled affair,
A rollercoaster of joy, angst & despair.
Yet beneath the squabbles, the sighs & the groans,
Lies laughter, redemption - and comfort in homes.

So here's to the bickering, the spats & the tiffs,
To eye-rolls, apologies & sarcastic riffs.
Relationships may fray, wobble & bend -
But with humour & heart - they're worth it. The end!!!

The Multitasking Magician: A Wandering Symphony

In this busy world, where tasks entwine,
A question arises, quite divine,
"*Can you multitask?*" they ask with flair,
To which I reply, with a sly little air:
"*Yeah, my friend, I've mastered the art,*
Of doing many things, right from the start,
I can listen to you, though my mind's astray,
Ignore your words & forget them all in a day!"
I've got the skill to juggle it all,
Like a performer in a comical hall,
While you speak your mind, I'll nod & smile,
But my thoughts may wander for quite a mile.
I'll hear your voice, like a distant song,
Yet in my mind, a melody plays along,
I'll nod and pretend to understand,
But my thoughts, my friend, they've got their own brand.
I'll ignore distractions, big or small,
Like a master of focus, I'll stand tall,
While chaos surrounds, I'll stay aloof,

In my own little world, under the same roof.
And as for remembering, oh, what a feat!
My mind's like a sieve, with a memory so fleet,
Your words may vanish, like a puff of smoke,
But worry not, my friend, it's just a little joke.
For in this grand graffiti of life,
Where moments are fleeting, like a butterfly's life,
I may forget the details, that's true,
But I'll remember the essence, the feelings I drew.
So yes, I can multitask, it's quite clear,
Though it may not be what you hold dear,
In this whimsical dance of listening, ignoring &
forgetting,
I find my own rhythm, without regretting.
So let us embrace this peculiar art,
With a wink, a chuckle & a hearty heart,
For in the chaos of life, let's not despair,
As we multitask & wander, without a care!!!

The Best People

They see the beauty in the world,
They feel the joy & pain,
They stand for what is right,
They fight against the rain.
They are the best of us,
The ones who make us proud,
They are the ones we follow,
The ones we look up to, without a doubt.
But they are also vulnerable,
They can be hurt & scarred,
They can be broken & defeated,
They can be torn apart.
So let us be kind to them,
Let us cherish them & love,
Let us protect them from the world,
Let us help them to be brave above.
For they are the best of us,
The ones who make us proud,
They are the ones we follow,
The ones we look up to, without a doubt!!!

Before My Time

I’ve seen what no child should see,
walked roads no boy should wander.
Life hit hard - unyielding, cruel -
my childhood splintered, left behind.
Under a sun that burned, not warmed,
I laboured, spirit aching,
feet worn on paths I never chose,
tasting defeat too bitter for youth.

Yet here I stand, head unbowed,
scarred by pain, shadowed by loss.
They linger - old companions -
but wisdom came with them, too.
My young years carry heavy truths,
fought for, won & seldom shared.
Other kids hold on to their innocence;
mine lies buried, quiet, unsmiling.

I am young, but my soul is old,
weathered by storms I never invited.

I’ve endured what breaks grown men,
and found strength waiting beneath.

A boy still lingers in this frame,
side by side with the man I became...

Scarred, but unbroken, heart beating on -
both surviving, both becoming anew!!!

Every Day, A Mother's Day

Yesterday, we celebrated -
flowers, cards, & warm words shared.
But love like hers isn't meant for a day.
It's an everyday kind of thing.
She raised us, nurtured us,
gave more than we'll ever know.
Her love wasn't seasonal,
so why should ours be?
For those whose mothers are gone,
their love still lingers, unfading.
Memory holds them close,
their spirit never leaves.
Let's honour them - all of them -
not just in marked moments,
but in the quiet, ordinary ones.
A mother's love never stops. Neither should ours.

Embracing Life's Dance: Notes to My Children

In life's wild tango, setbacks do appear,
But sitting defeated is what we mustn't adhere.
The present may pout, wearing gloom like a shroud,
Yet the future holds secrets, vibrant & proud.
Quirky & light, the human path we tread,
A dance of contradictions, where hopes are fed.
Challenges arise, with laughter we defy,
In the comedy of life, we find reasons to fly.
My dear children, just ponder this rhyme,
A personal ode to the ebb & flow of time.
Embrace the absurdity, let resolve take flight,
For in life's merry waltz, we'll find pure delight!!!

On Wings of Rhyme & Reason

I take flight on paper wings
Thru' endless nights
A soul unbound
By the constraints of time
Truth unveiled in verse -
Crisp, chiming...

Havens built of books
Ink & dreams
Where timeless tales
Gleam in cadence
Of brave heroes
And lovers doomed to part
Each page a canvas
Revealing life's art

With words, I paint the world
In vivid hues
From sunrise dawns

To twilight's gentle dews
I capture laughter,
Tears
And all that lies
Within human hearts
And skies

For life - a whispered song
Fleeting, fragile
Upon the wind's swift wing
Yet thru' my woven words
Its essence thrives
A legacy
That time cannot erode
But will forevermore abide

Let me take wing
On reason & rhyme
Thru' knowledge
In each season
My spirit takes flight
Verse eternally etched
For all time!!!

Unrequited

The light in your eyes lifted me skyward,
A winter's end, I thought, spring beginning.
Those early days - dizzy heights,
Your words, perfect melodies.

Then clouds gathered.
I learned too late your heart remained your own.
I inspired poetry in my soul,
But not in yours.

From elation to grey despair,
Grasping at thin air,
Struggling to turn your gaze
Toward my unconquered feeling.

Weeping, bargaining, fury, pride -
Nothing swayed your staunch refrain.
My ardour locked outside in the rain.

In the ember-twilight of what we were,

I mourn what might have been.
Hopes scattered like ashes,
Blown by fickle winds.

Yet love flickers still,
Its genuine heat endures
Even against harsh denial.

I shall treasure in my chest
These memories of emotions,
A bittersweet song of roads not taken.

Two hearts never harmonising their glory,
Playing different melodies.
Yet as our rhythms scatter,
My love remains intact.

You, my eternal muse, my hopeless desire -
This verse exalts the undying fire
That continues to flicker
At love's conquered shrine!!!

Peak to Valley: The Journey

I stand on the mountain's peak,
wind rushing, alive in my lungs.
Clouds below, sun above -
a moment of pure, golden light.

But the valley calls, so I climb down,
feet stumbling on winding trails.
Shadows dance, rivers roar,
scraped knees, heart racing fast.

The sun dips, just out of sight.
Cold & tired, I keep going.
A clearing appears - hope sparks.
Is this the end? Nope, just a new turn!

Streams whisper secrets to me:
endings are just new starts in disguise.
The sun bursts thru', fierce & bright,
and my heart soars with its warmth.

Valleys behind me, new peaks ahead.
Life keeps rolling, bitter & sweet,
joy & regret, chaos & calm -
a wild, never-ending tune.

The kid inside me still watches,
amazed by the world's loud, messy song.
Up, down, around each bend,
the road keeps going, no end in sight.

We're still becoming who we're meant to be.
Still becoming - always, **endlessly!!!**

IT IS SO

Life doesn't knock.
It kicks the door in,
strips you down,
and tosses you into the current -
no safety net, no applause, no lifeguard on duty!

It doesn't care who you are.
Decorated veteran, corporate warrior,
dreamer, builder, survivor -
the water doesn't ask for your résumé.

You can fight it.
Claw at the waves, scream at the sky,
curse the river for flowing without your permission.
But the current doesn't flinch.

Or -
you can let go.
Let the water take you,
bones rattling, lungs burning,

but still... moving forward.

It won't be graceful.
You'll hit rocks.
Your pride will wash up somewhere downstream,
soaking wet & unrecognisable.

But the river never cared for your pride anyway.

Feel it all - the fear, the rage, the ache.
Let the cold water slap you awake,
remind you you're still breathing.
Still here!

'Coz life doesn't owe you comfort.
It owes you nothing -
except the next sunrise.

So, scream, sink, swim - hell, float face down for a bit if you must.
But don't ask why.
Don't wait for rescue.

Just move!

Because the river won't stop.
And neither will you!

IT IS SO!!!

The Language of Kindness

Kindness is a language
That transcends all barriers.
It can be spoken
In words, in deeds,
In gestures,
In looks.

It can be heard
By the deaf,
And seen
By the blind.

It is a melody
That soothes the soul,
A symphony
That fills the heart with joy.

It is a language
That unites us all,
A gift

That we can all share.

So, let us speak kindness
To one another,
And let us spread kindness
To the world.

Together,
We can make the world
A kinder place!!!

Tale of the Infinite

From timeless depths, I've watched worlds rise & fall,
My fiery gaze the locus of all life.
I've nurtured seedlings, coaxed the tides to dance,
And painted skies with hues beyond compare.
Millennia have passed beneath my watch,
I've seen the folly & the strength of man.
Great empires crumble, new ones take their place,
While I remain, unchanged, *yet ever-changing.*
My gravity binds planets in their paths,
My light illumes the darkest cosmic night.
I birth the seasons with my steady march,
And reason bows before my ancient might.
Yet in the vastness of the universe,
I'm but a speck, a fleeting spark of fire.
Still, on this fragile orb I hold so dear,
My presence marks the boundary of all.
From dawn to dusk, from pole to equator,
I've choreographed the dance of dark & light.
I've witnessed beauty, terror, love & turmoil,
The endless cycle of decay & growth.

My essence flows thru' every living thing,
A golden thread in life's grand fabric.
I am the alpha & omega here,
The source of warmth, of hope, of time itself!

Behold my glory, tremble at my power -
I am the Orange Orb!!!

The Last Horizon - A Captain's Bow

This is where the sky bends low,
where the ocean hums its oldest song,
and the wind carries whispers
of lands I've left behind.

I have walked thru' forests
that remember the footsteps of giants,
crossed deserts where the sun
wrote poems in the sand.
I have stood on cliffs
where the sea roared its defiance,
and in quiet villages
where time folded itself into stillness.

The world is a mosaic of stories -
each face a map,
each voice a compass
pointing to some uncharted truth.
I have gathered them like seashells,

held them to my ear,
and heard the echo of my own pulse.

My verses found rhythm not in rhyme,
but in the staggered breath of living -
free, untamed, unmetered.
A map of moments sketched in ink and memory,
a passport stamped with feelings, not borders.

Now, at the edge of this journey,
I see the horizon stretch itself wide,
a canvas waiting for the next brushstroke.
The poems I've written are not endings,
but bridges -
each one a step toward the infinite.

So I leave this book as a lantern,
its light flickering with the colours -
of all I've seen and felt.
Take it with you,
and may it guide you
to your own horizon -

Because there will always be another poem.
Another shore.
Another sunrise
that doesn't need rhyming to be beautiful.

And I will write it -
one breath, one heartbeat,
one untamed word at a time!!!

9 789369 53024

Printed by Libri Plureos GmbH in Hamburg, Germany